I0496856

This Book Belongs To

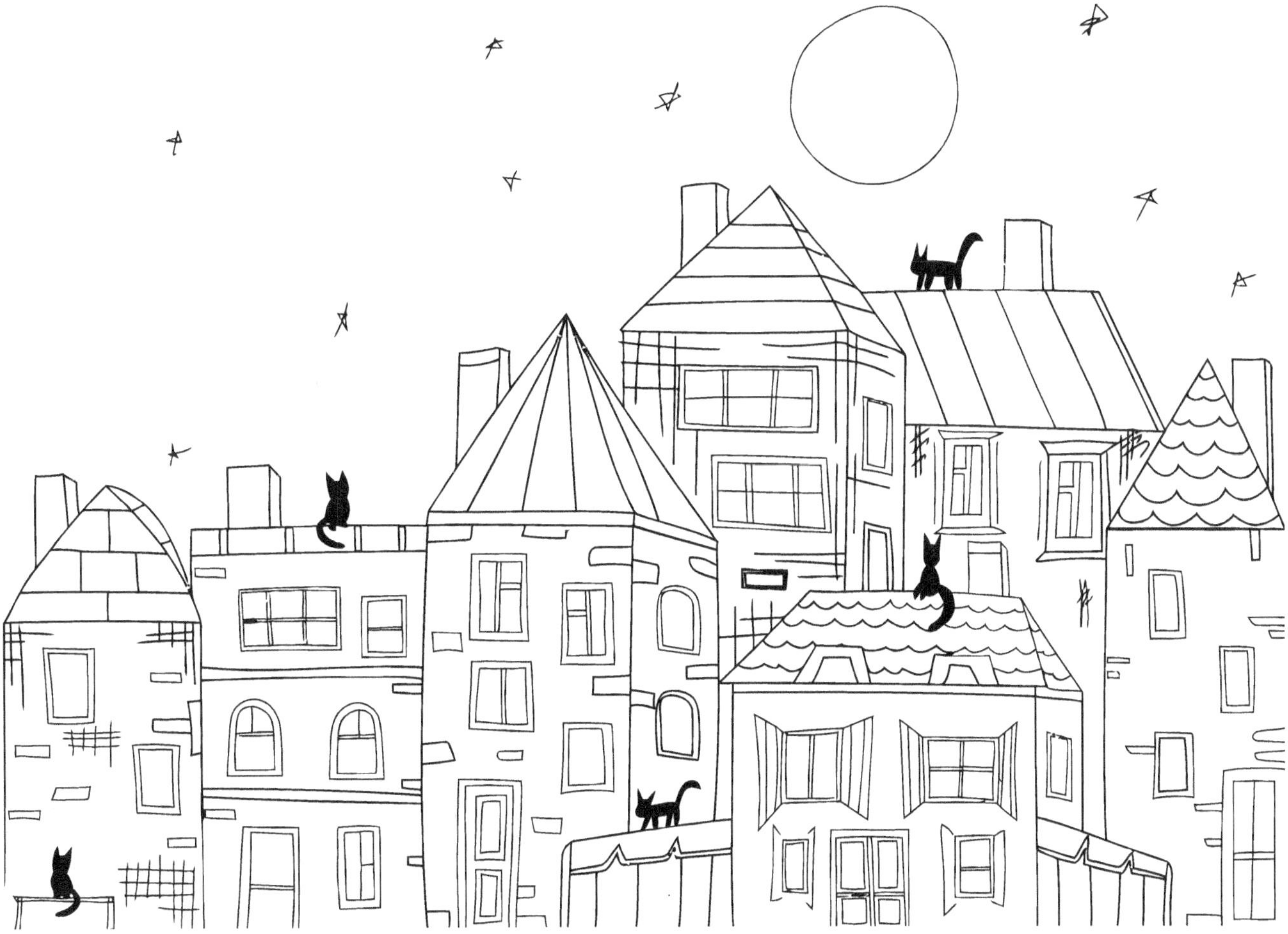

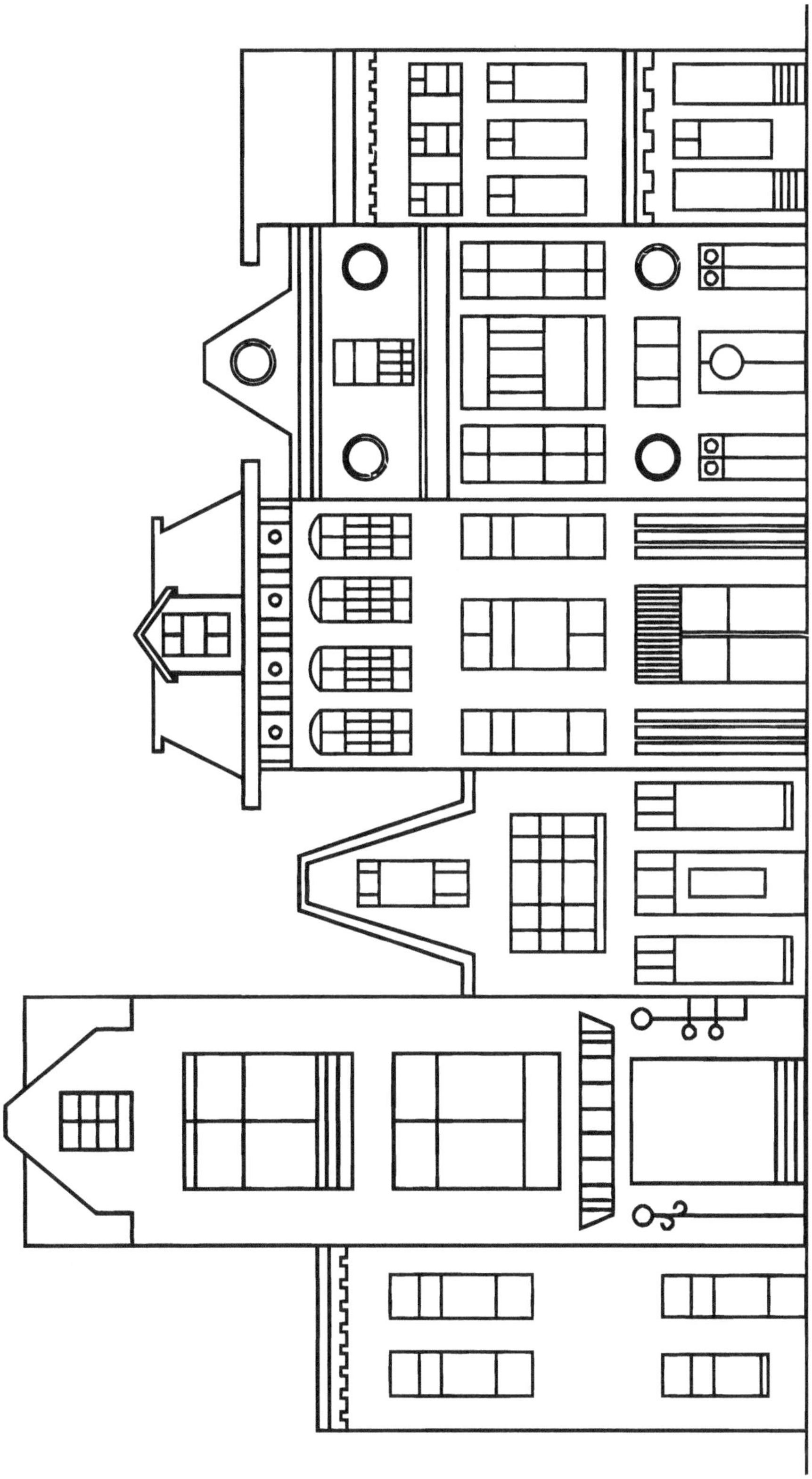

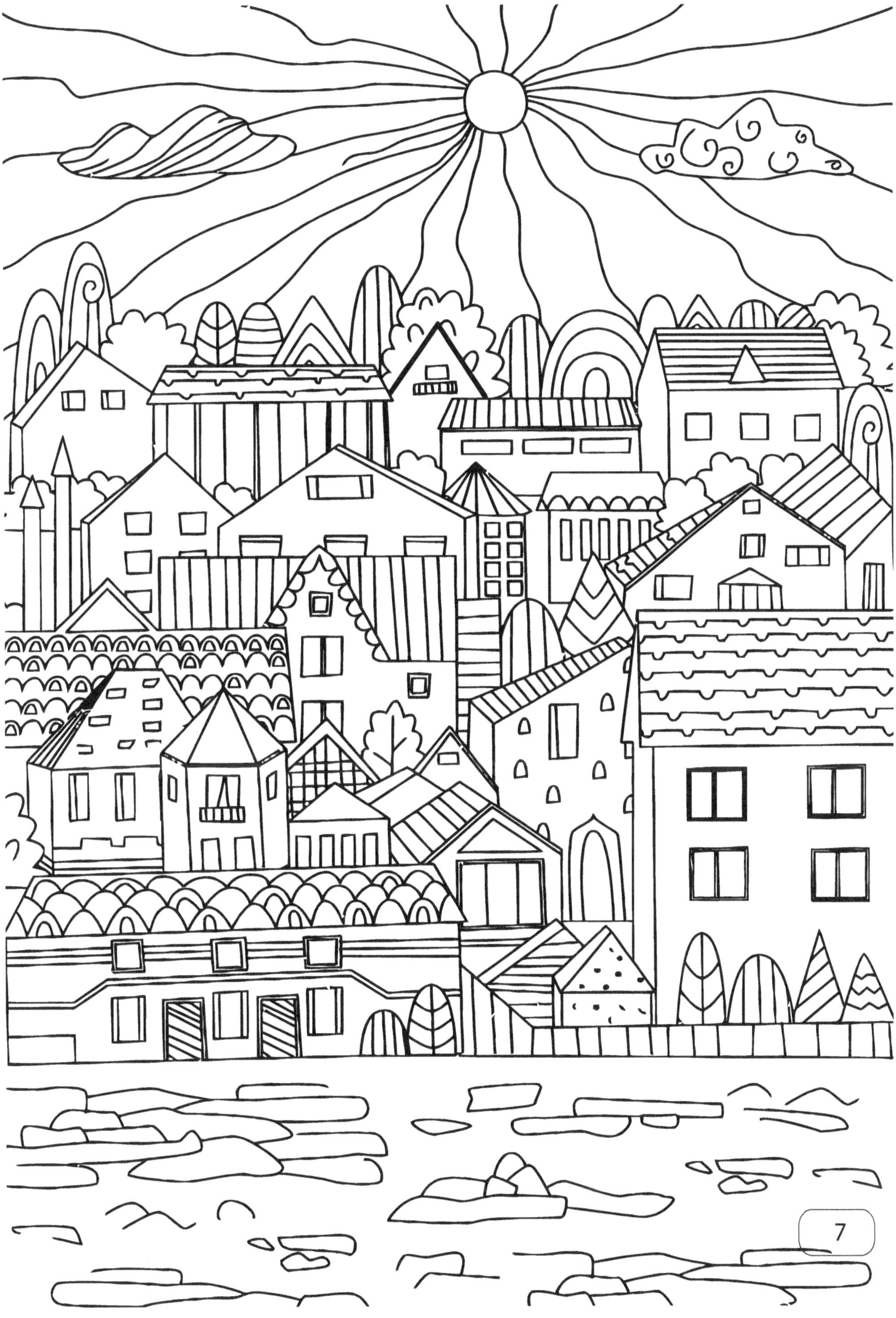

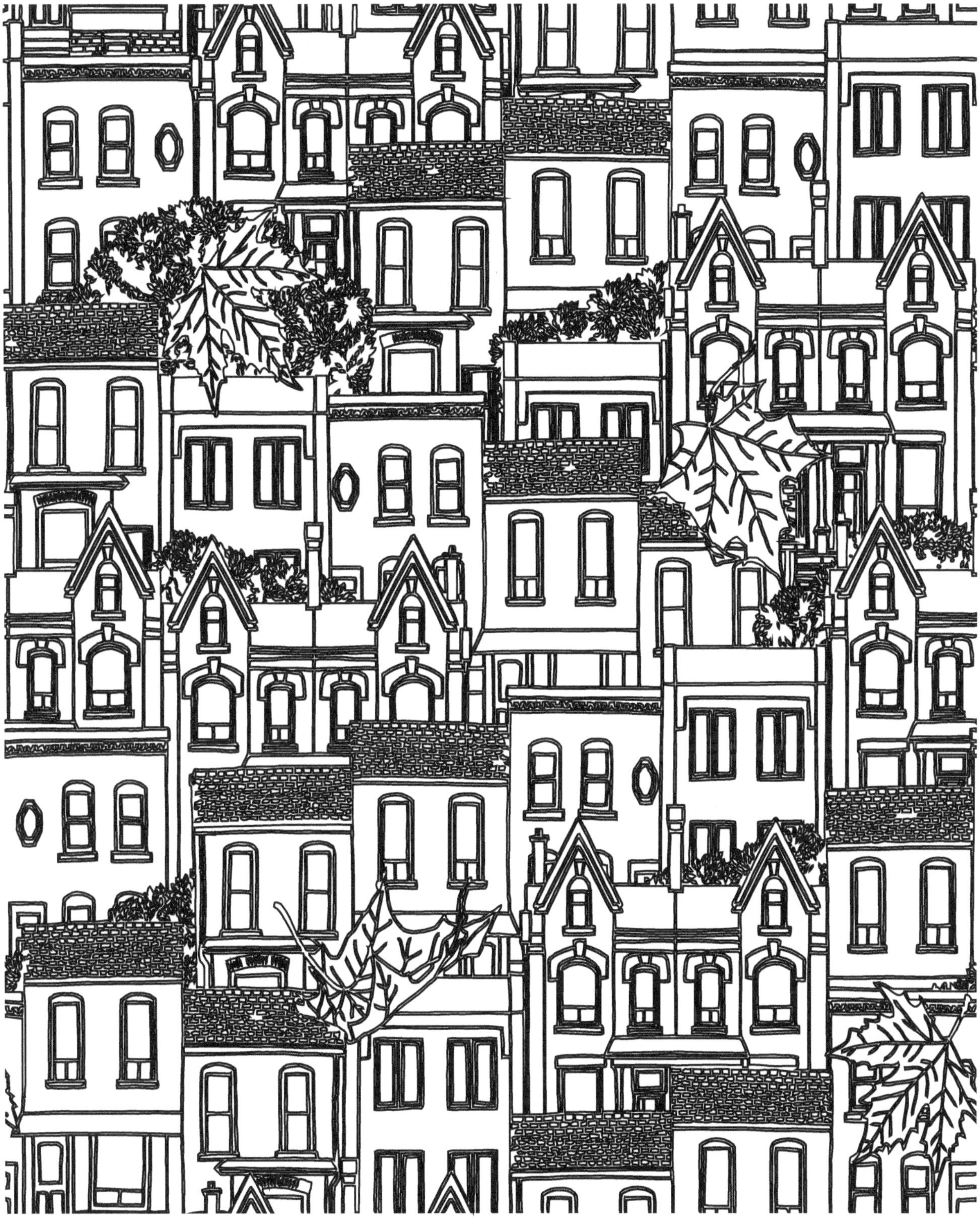

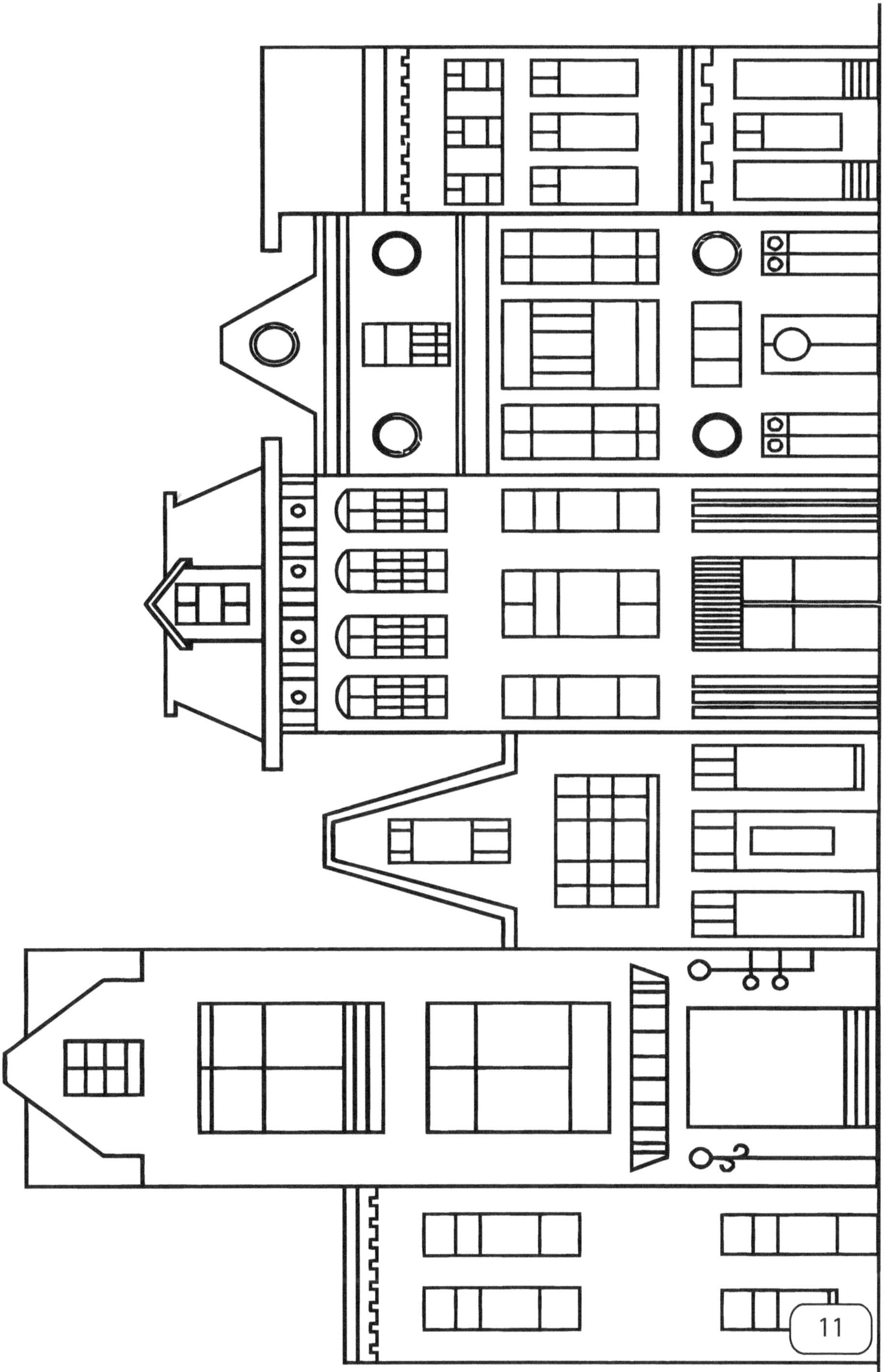

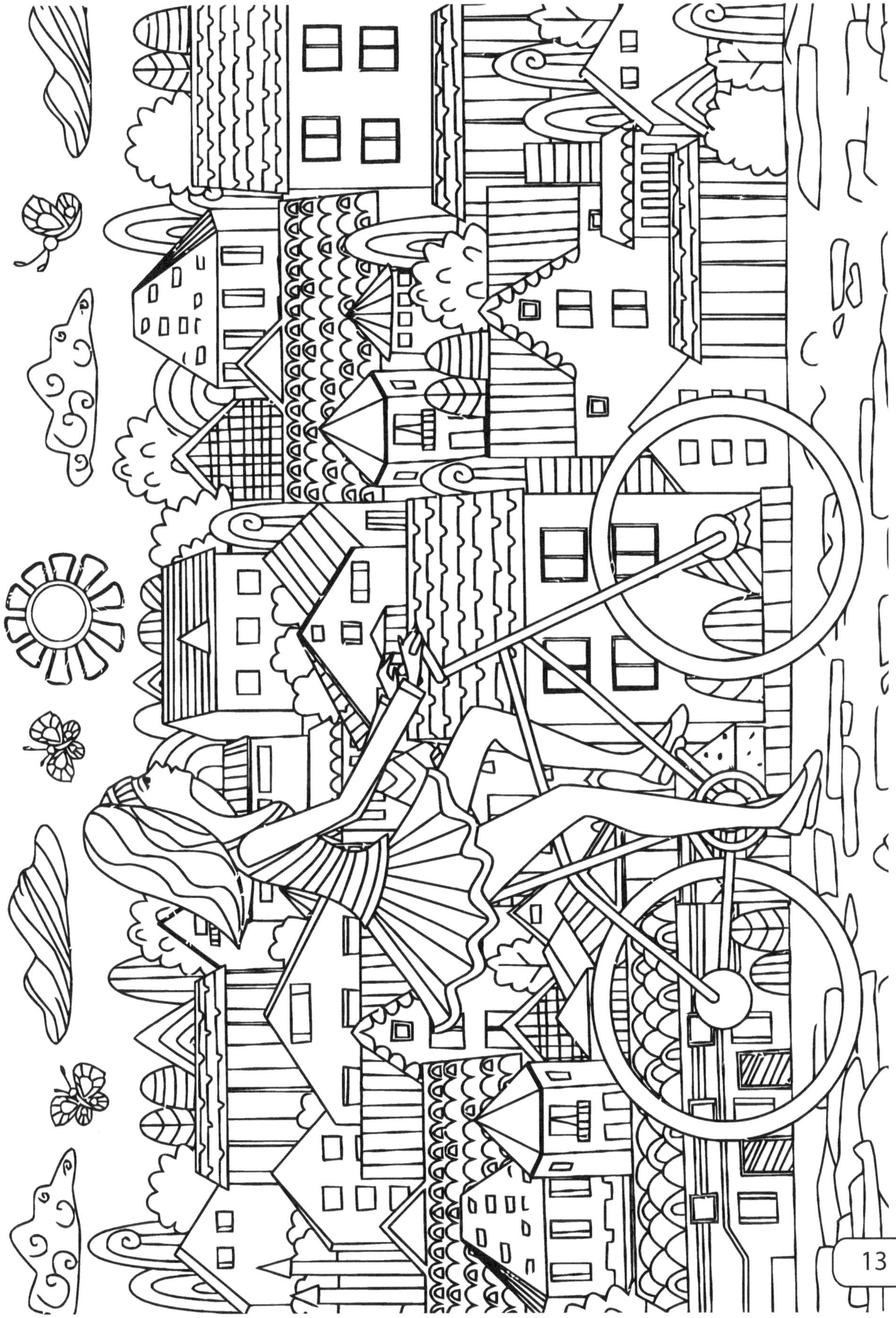

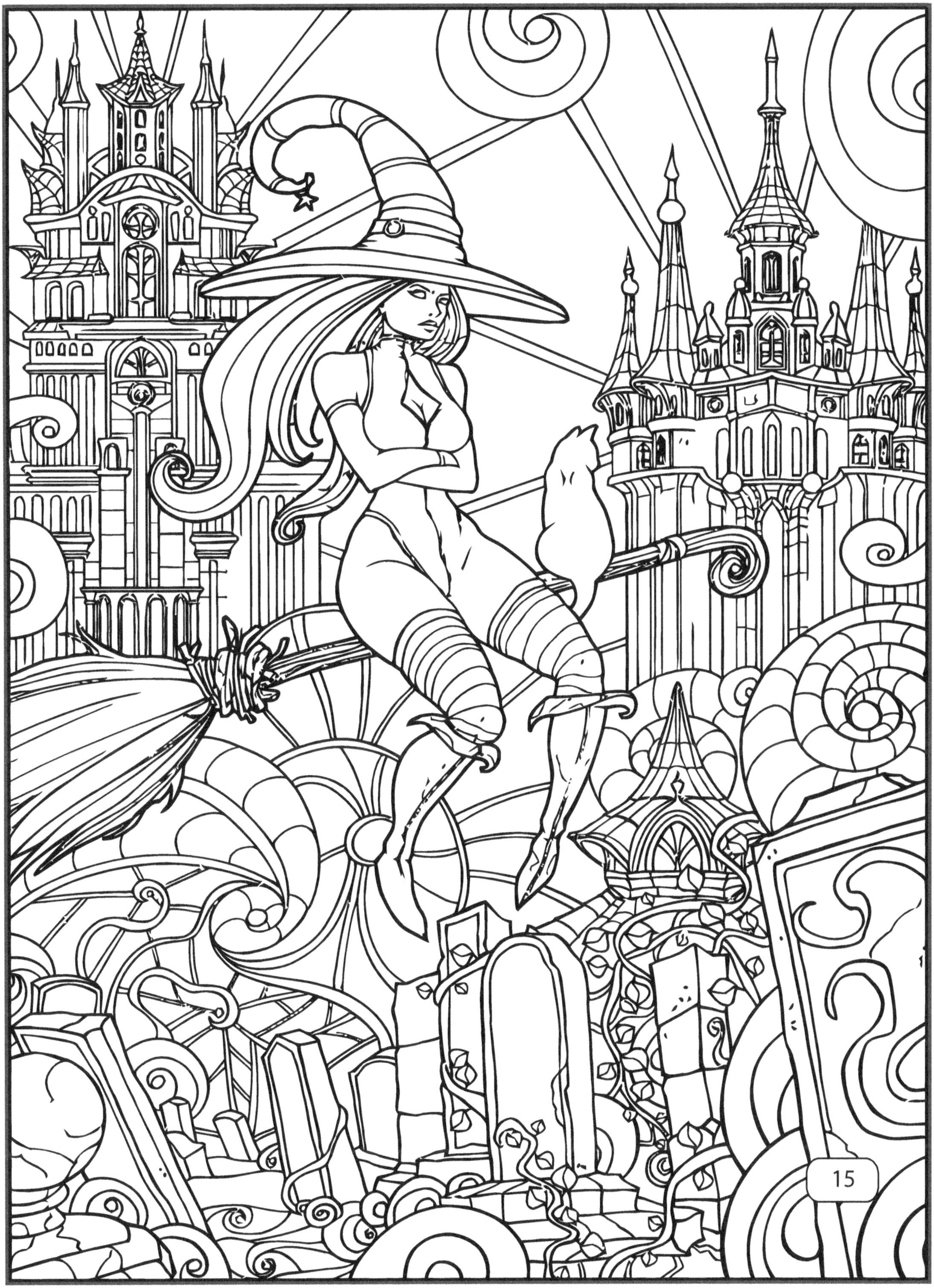

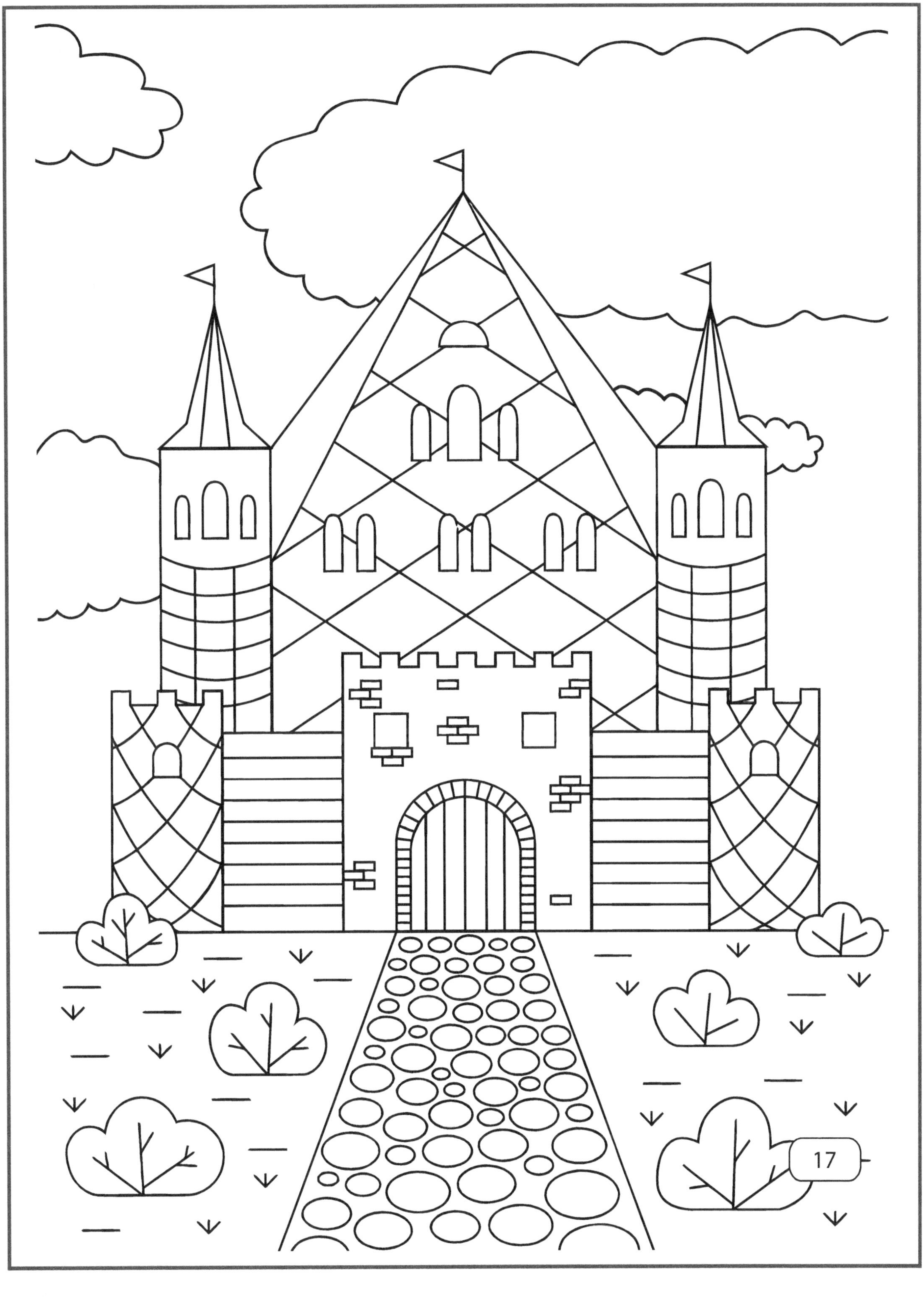

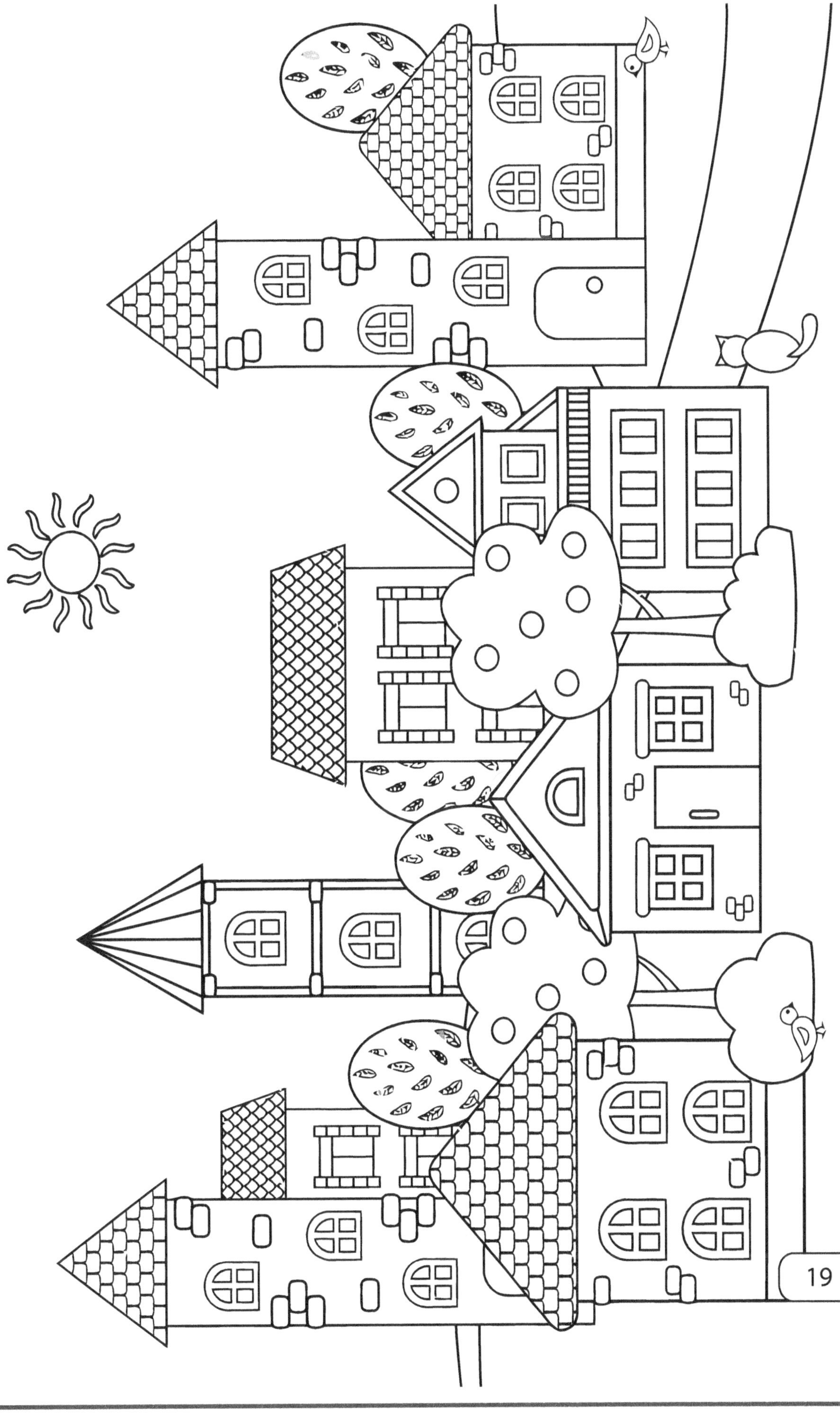

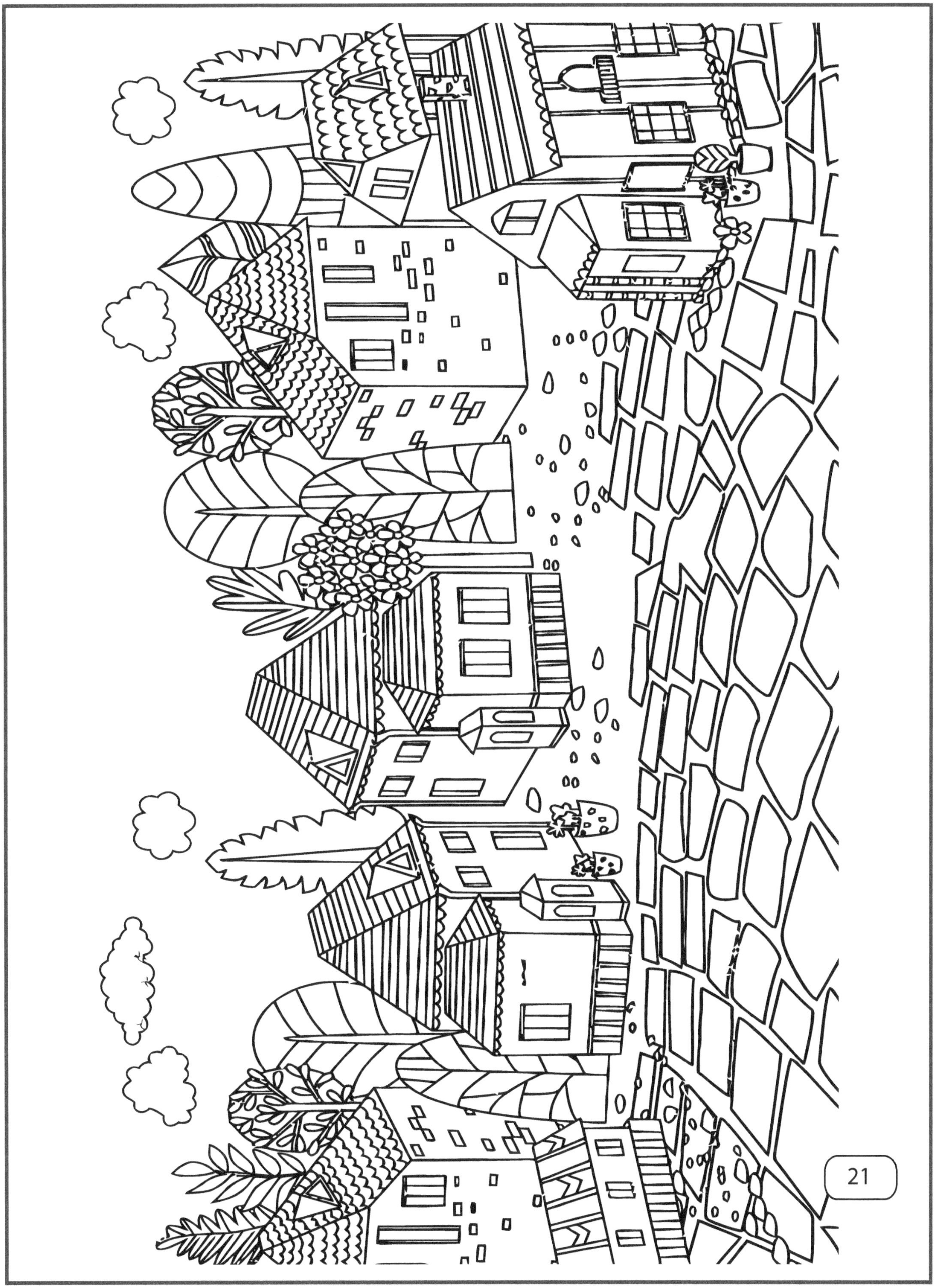

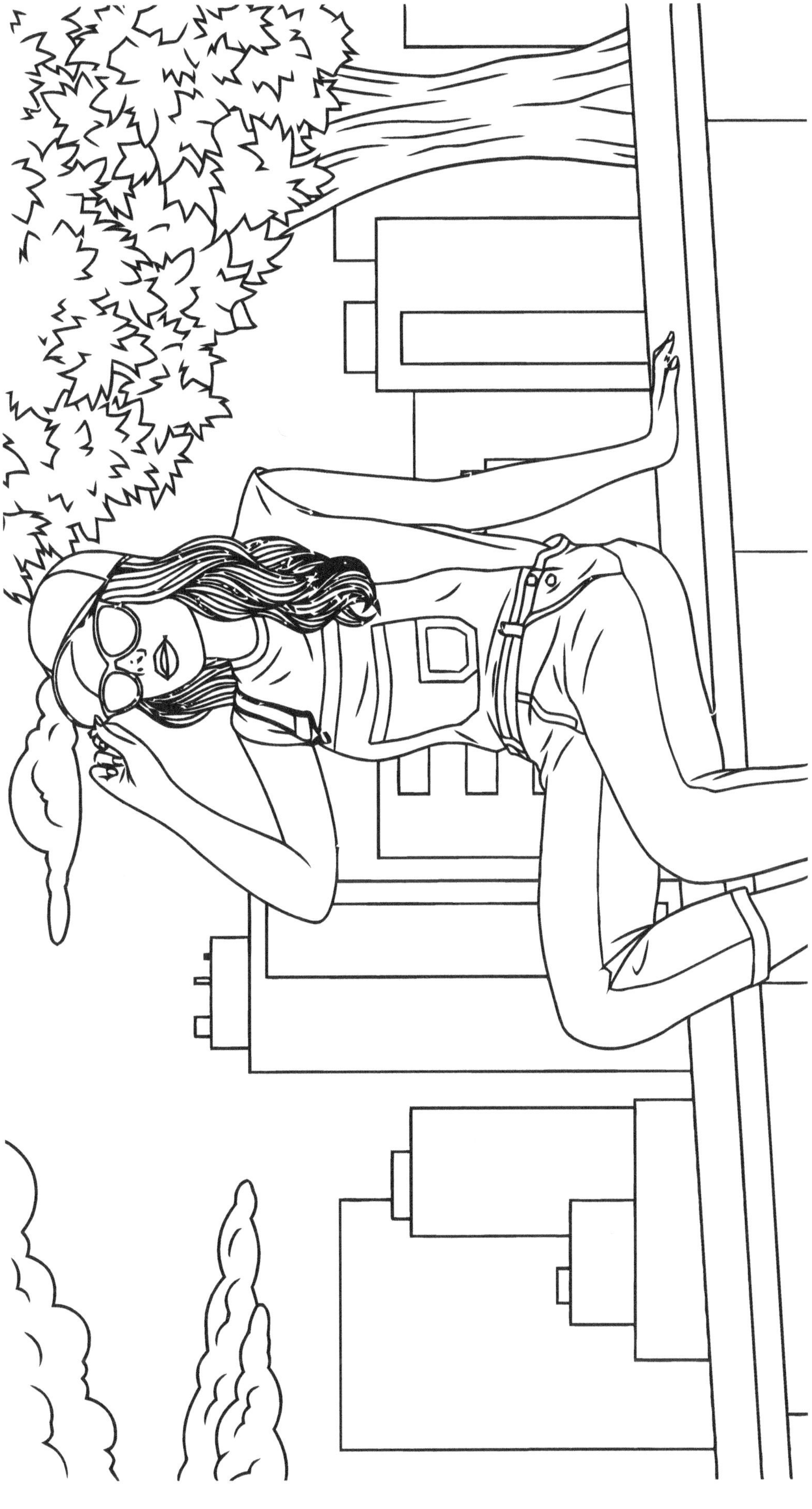

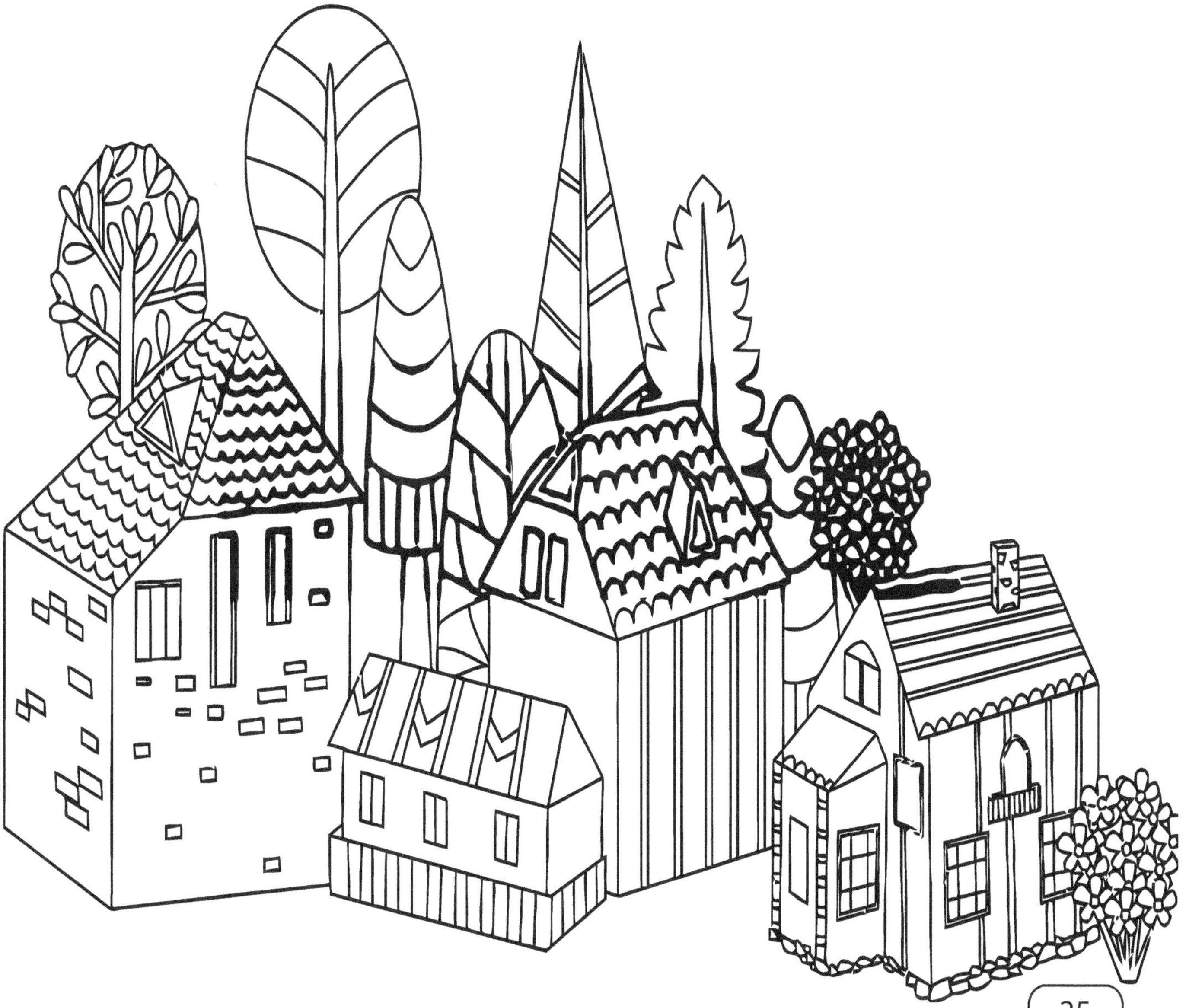

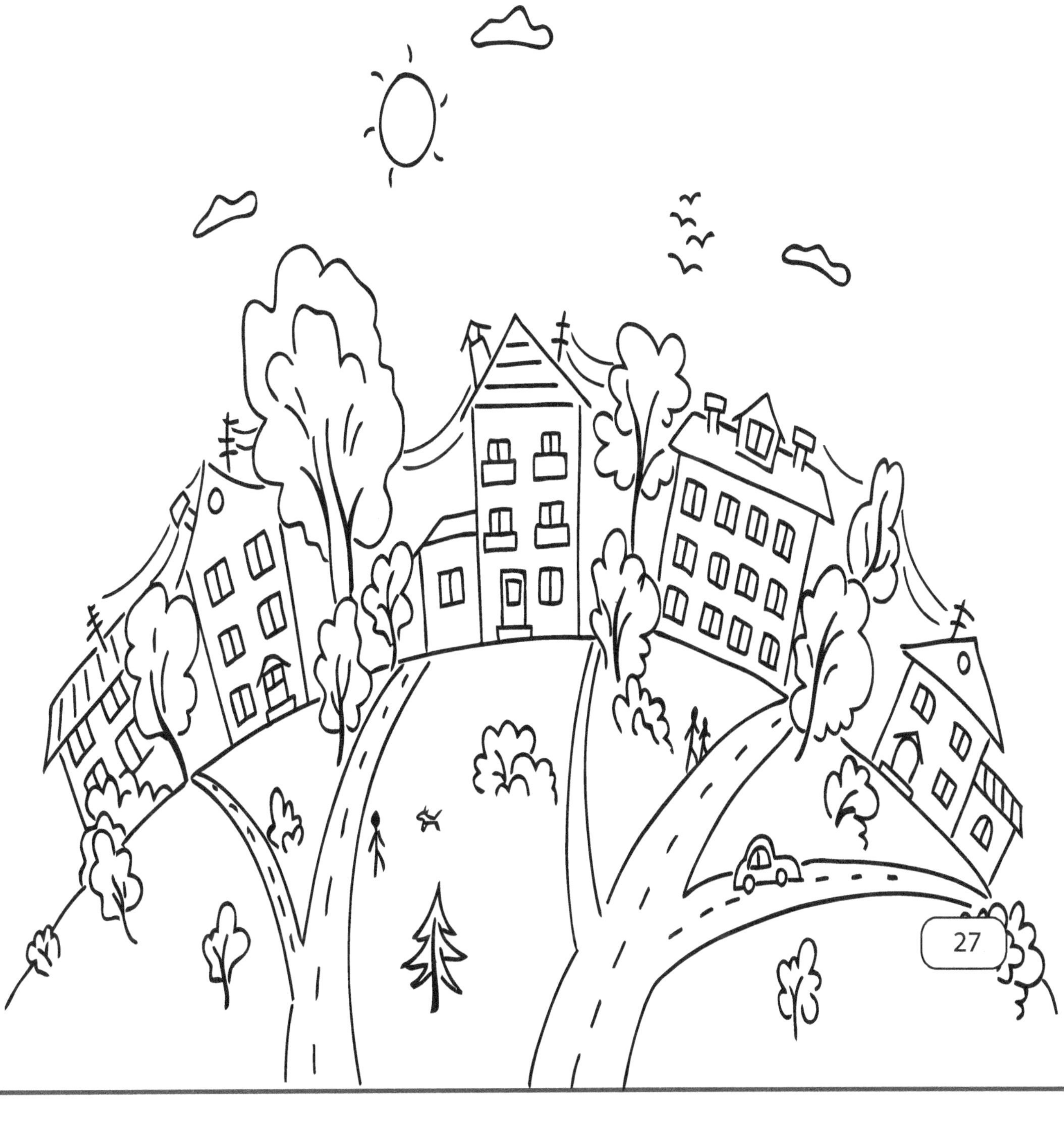

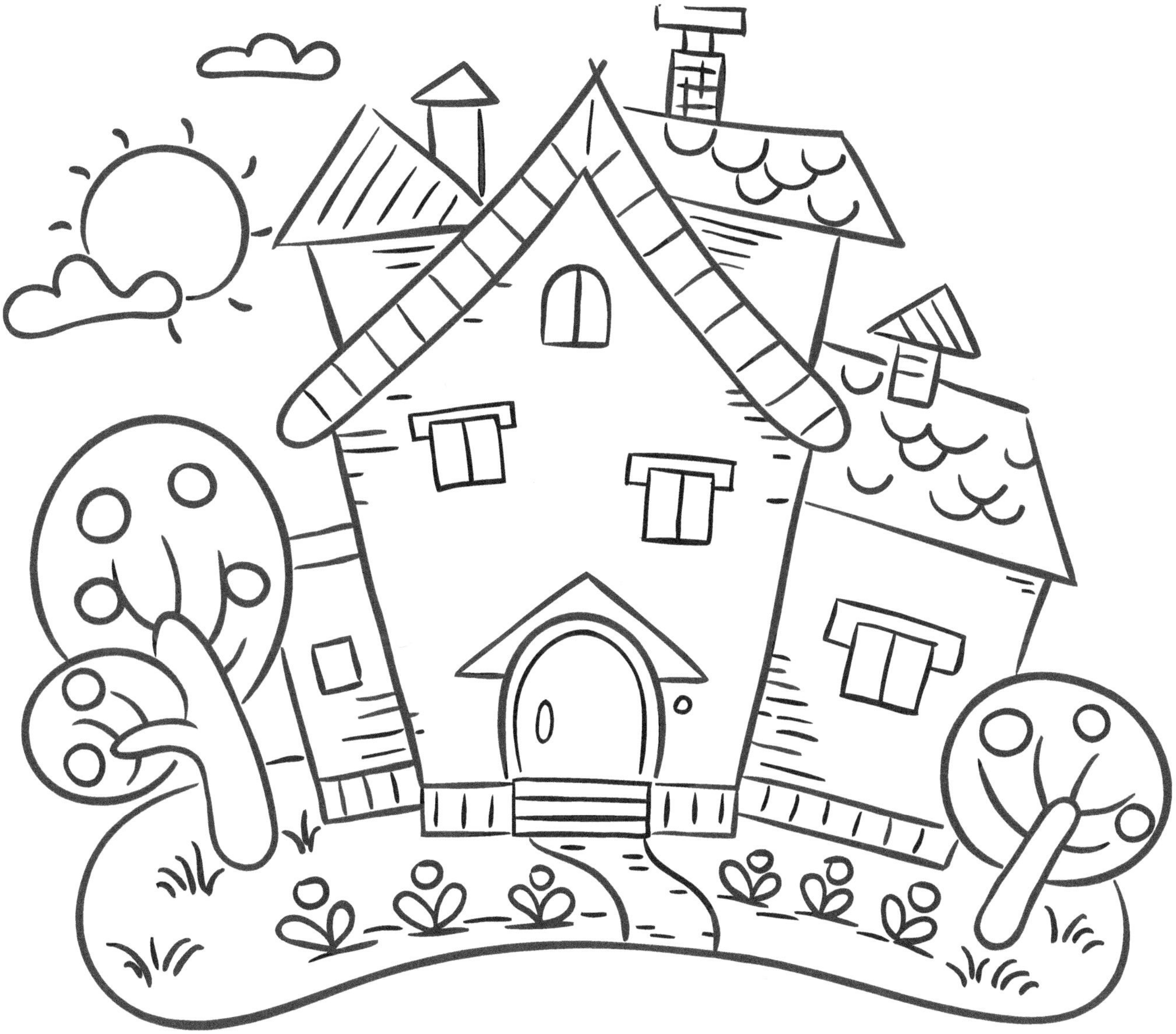

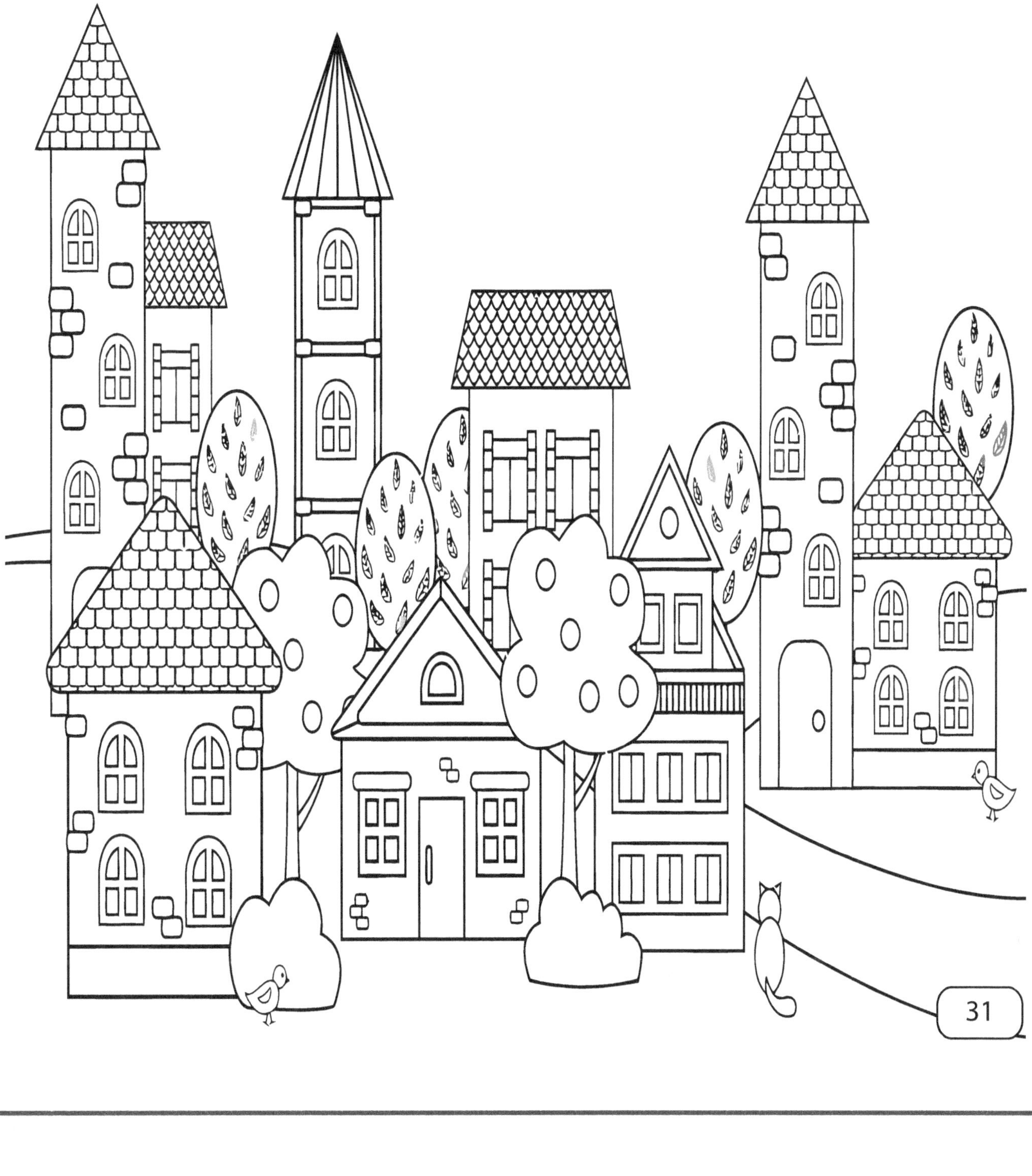

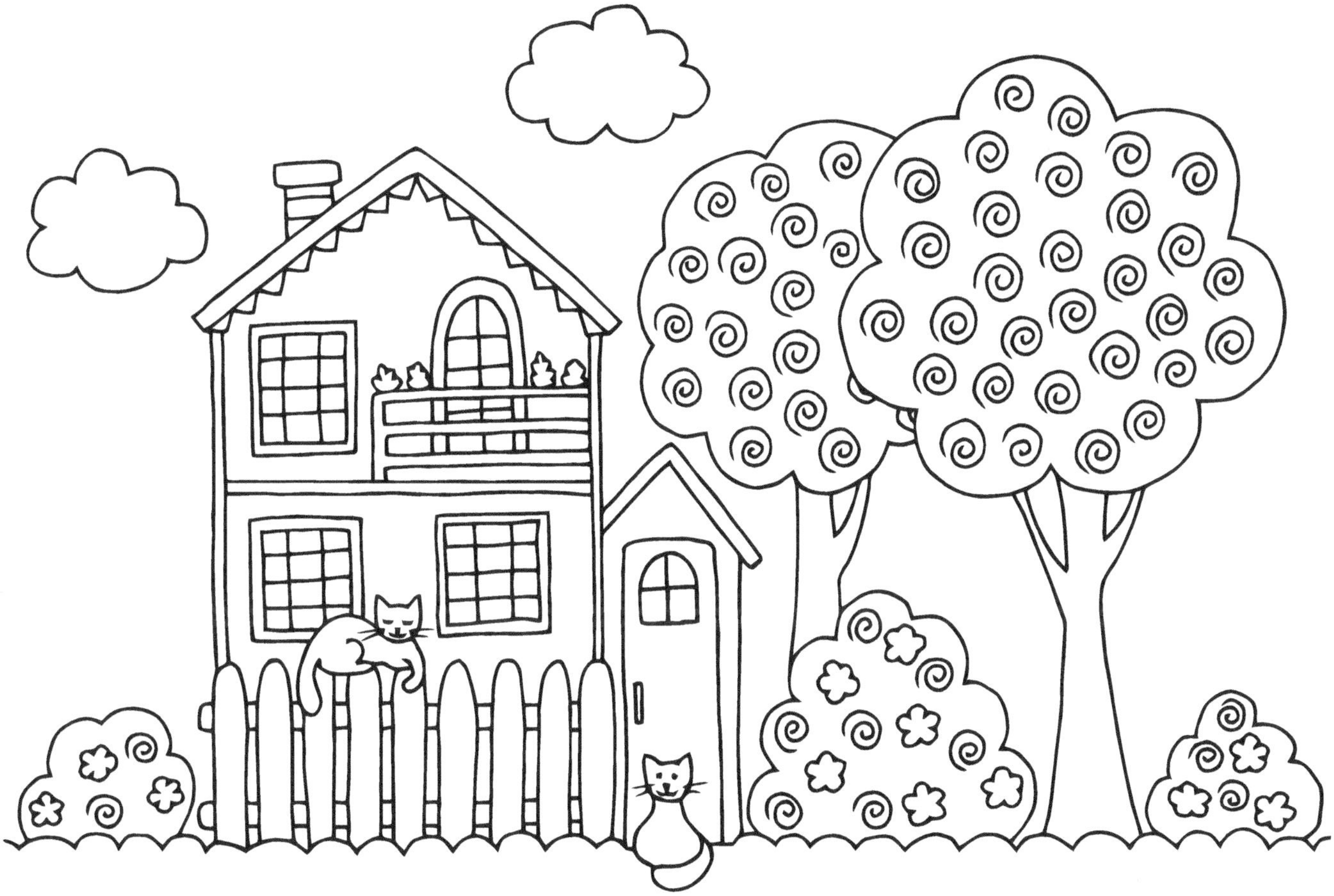

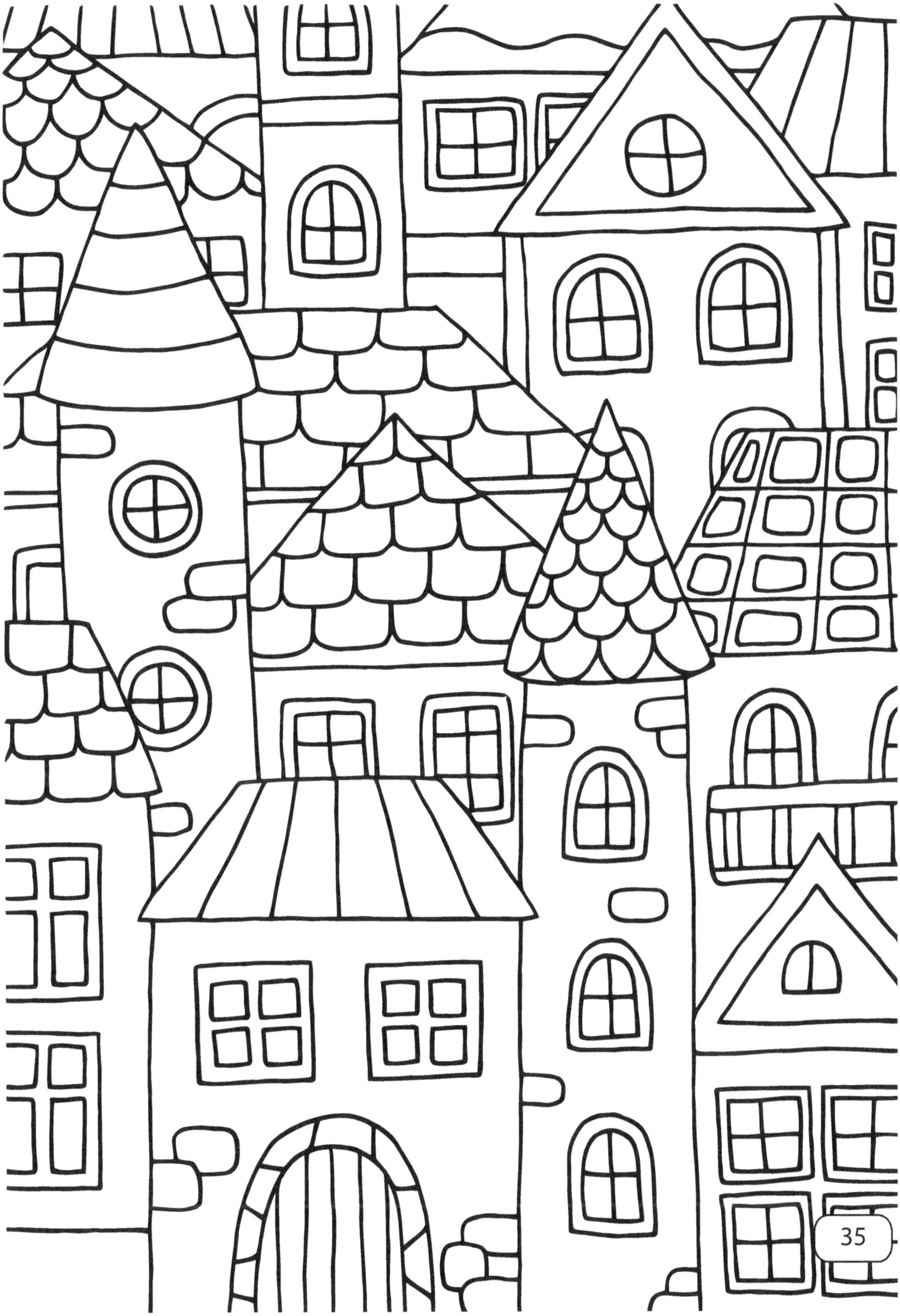

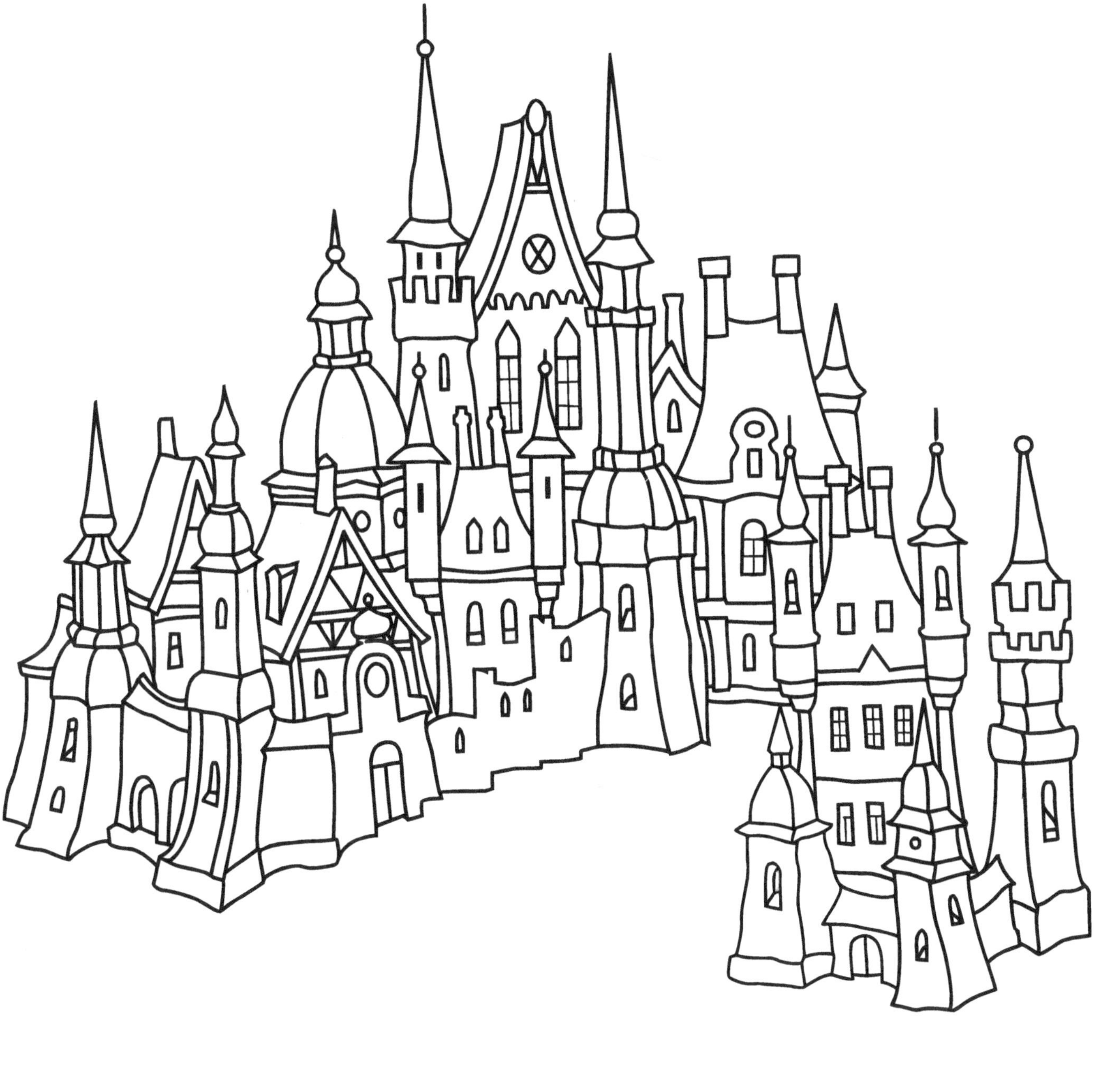

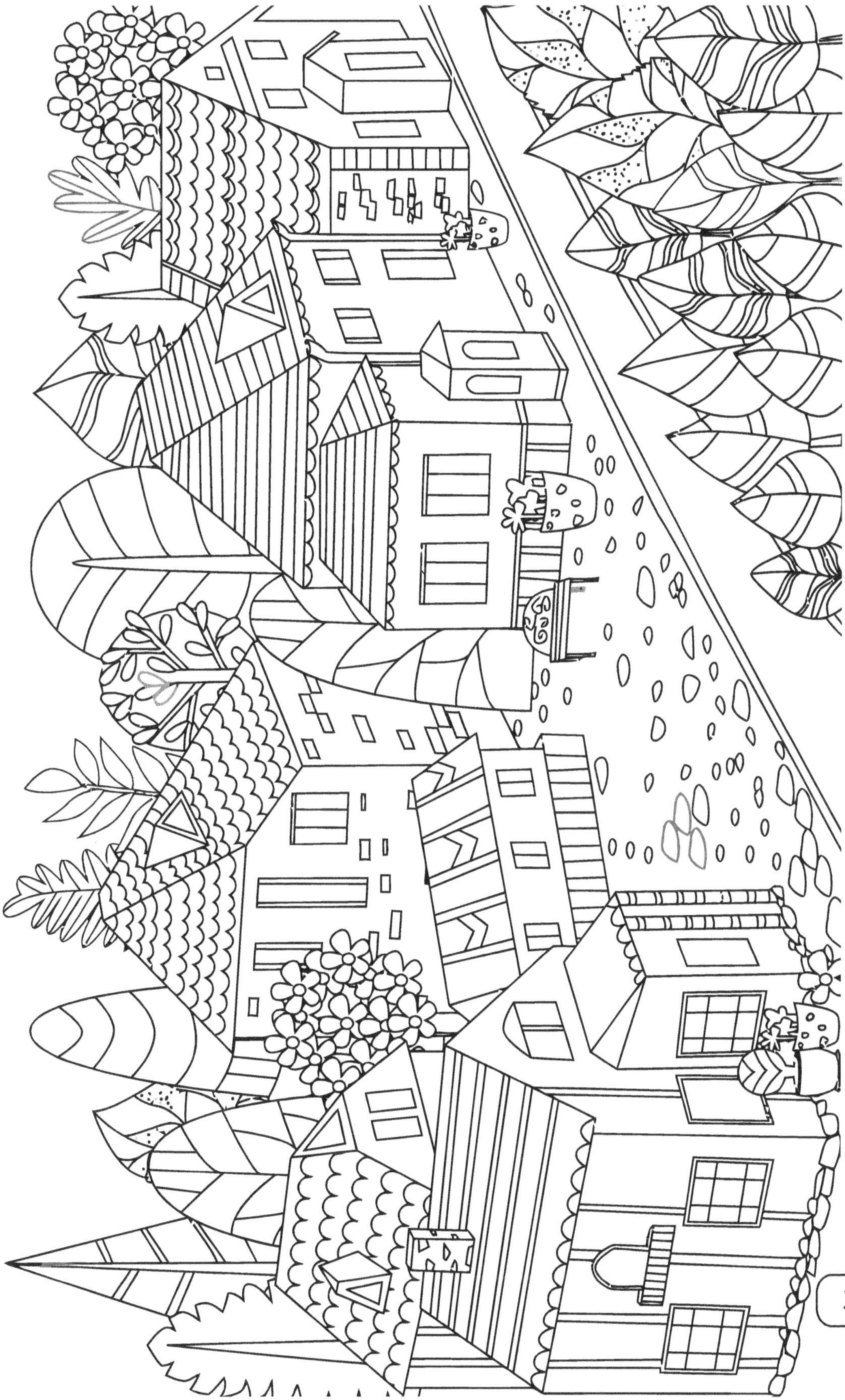

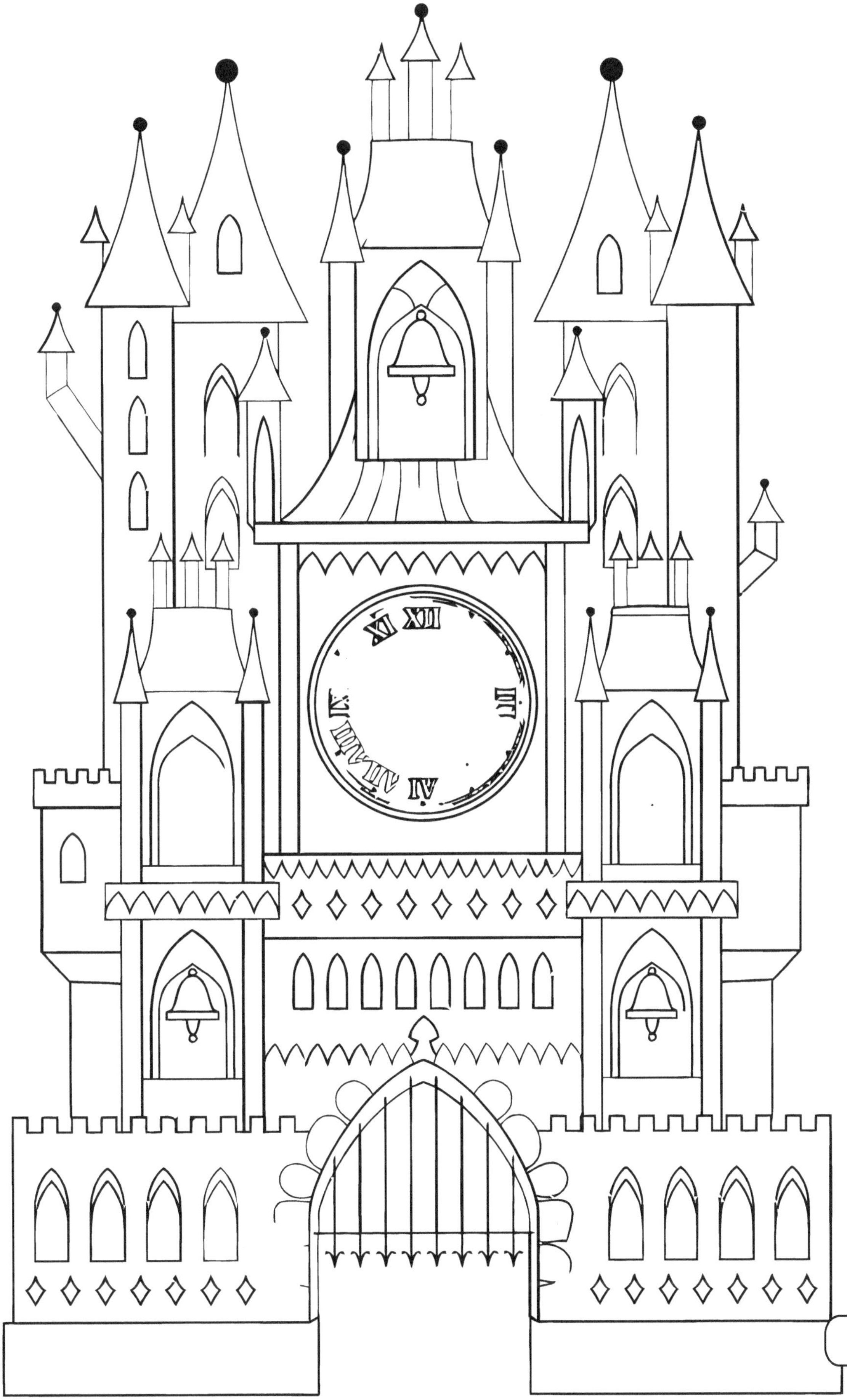

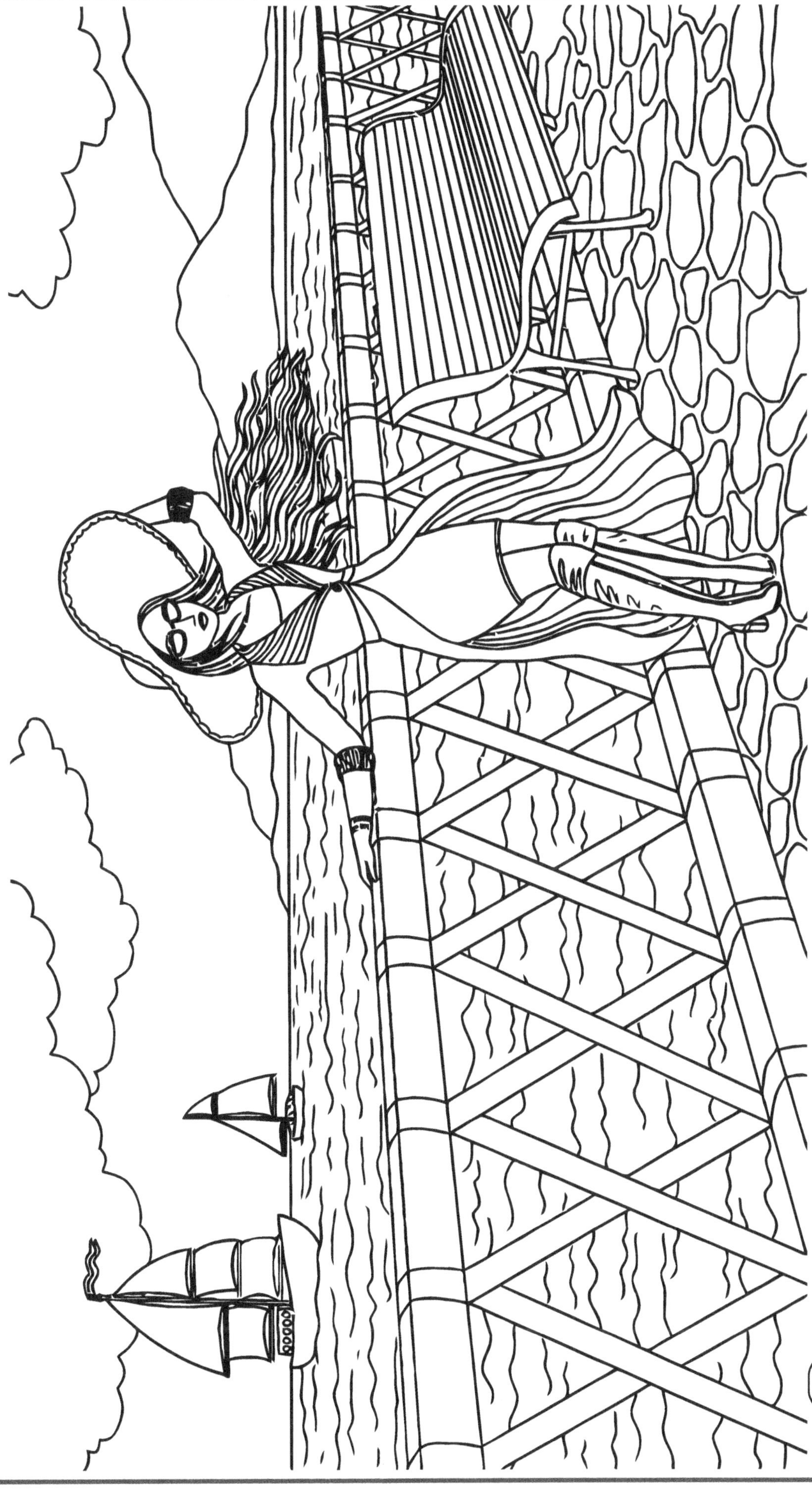

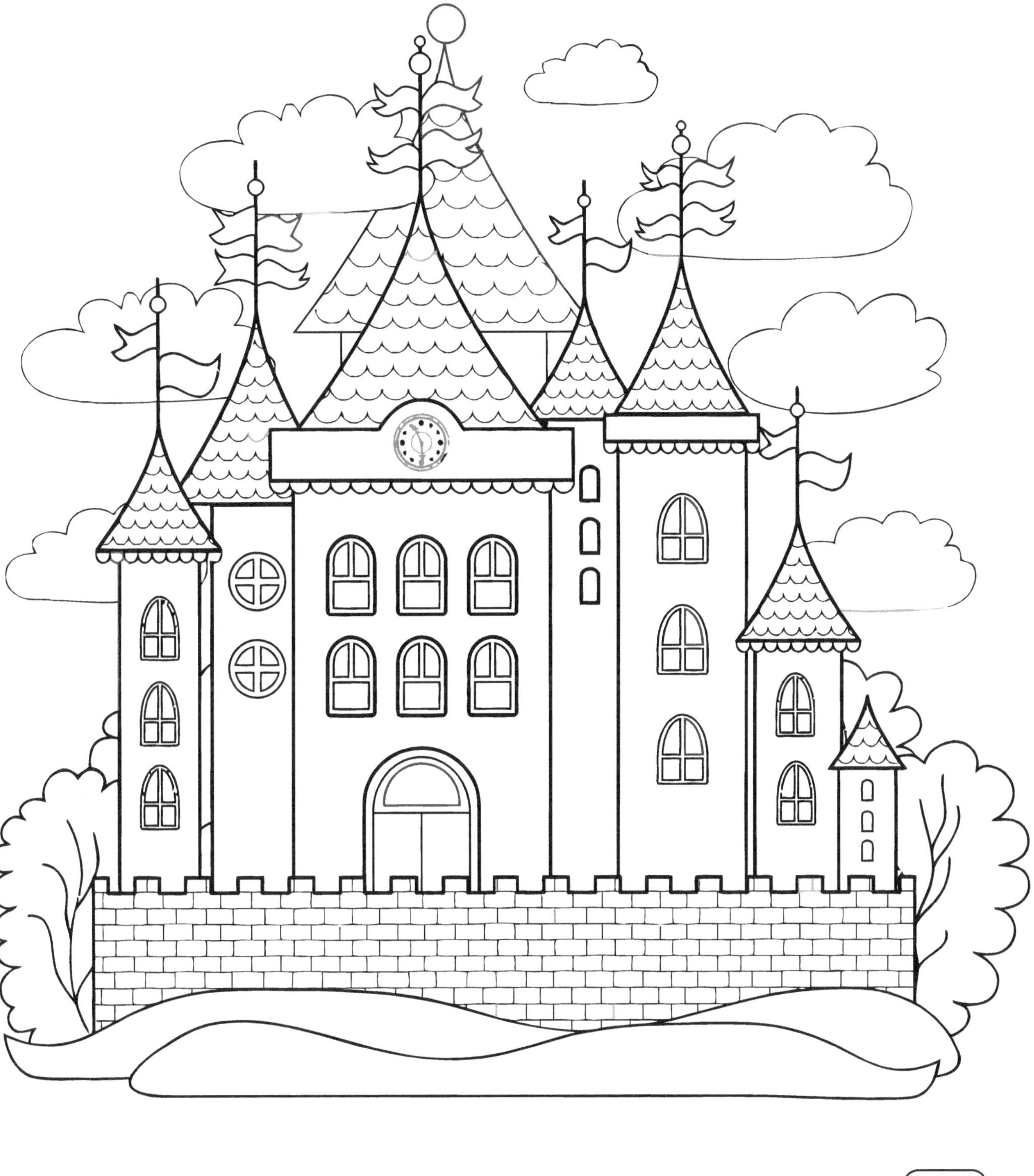

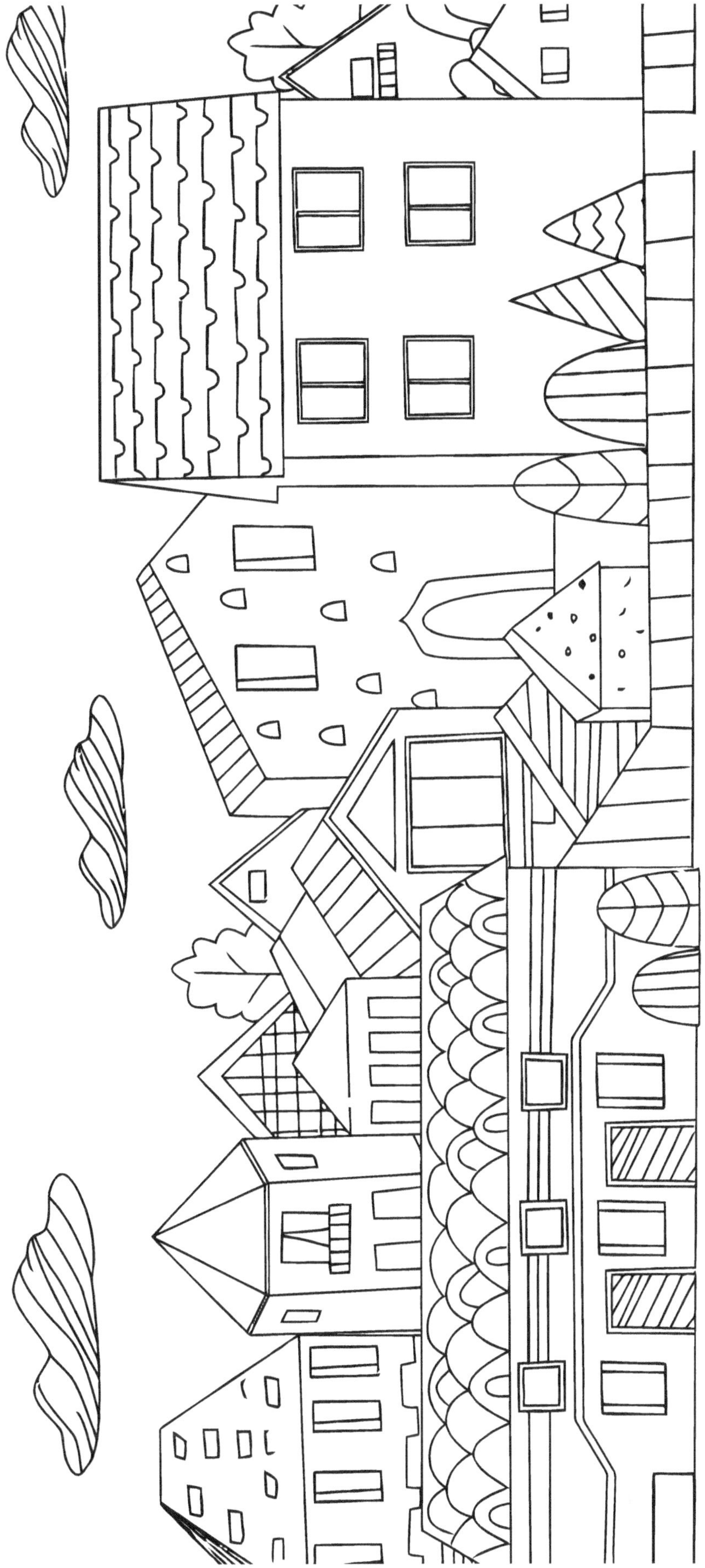

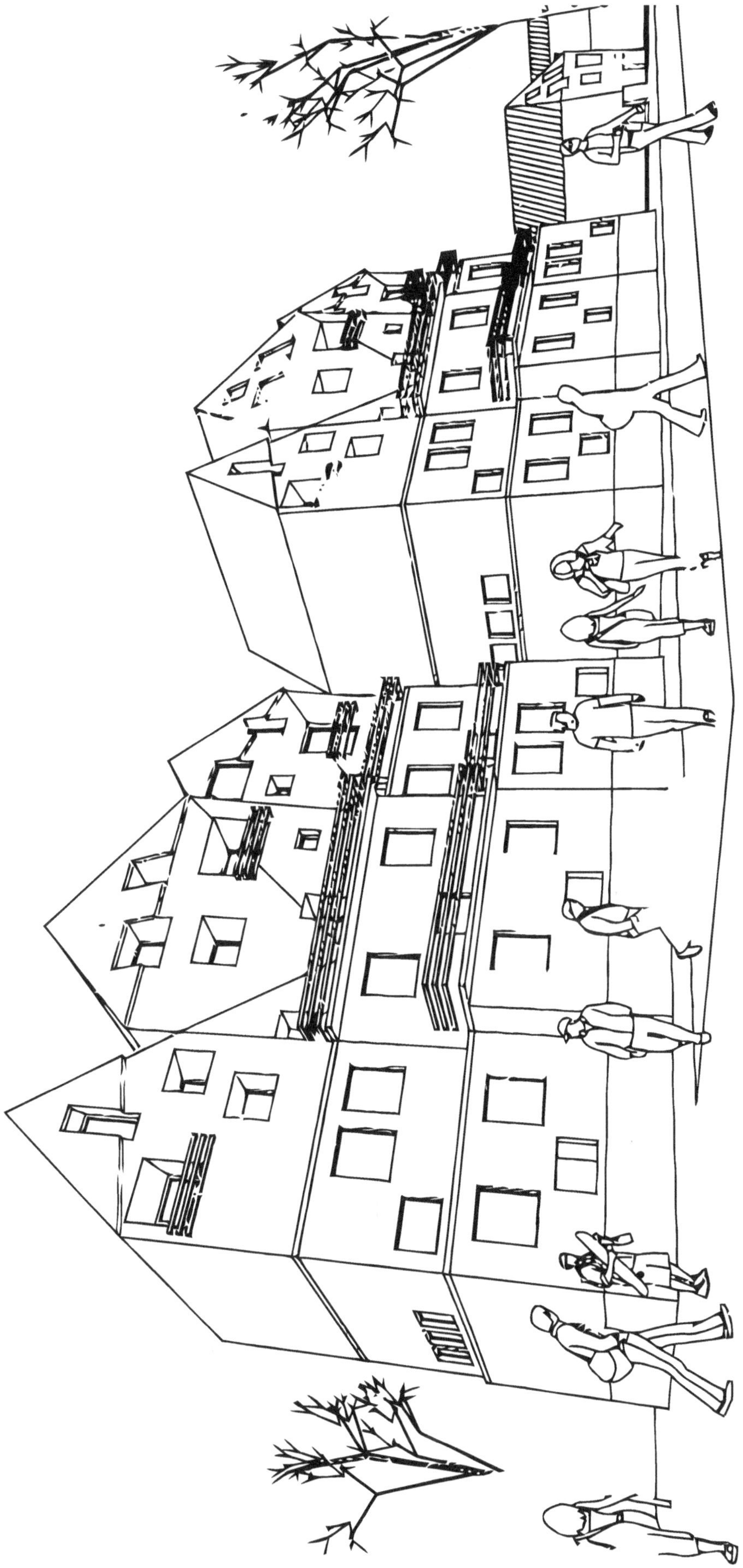

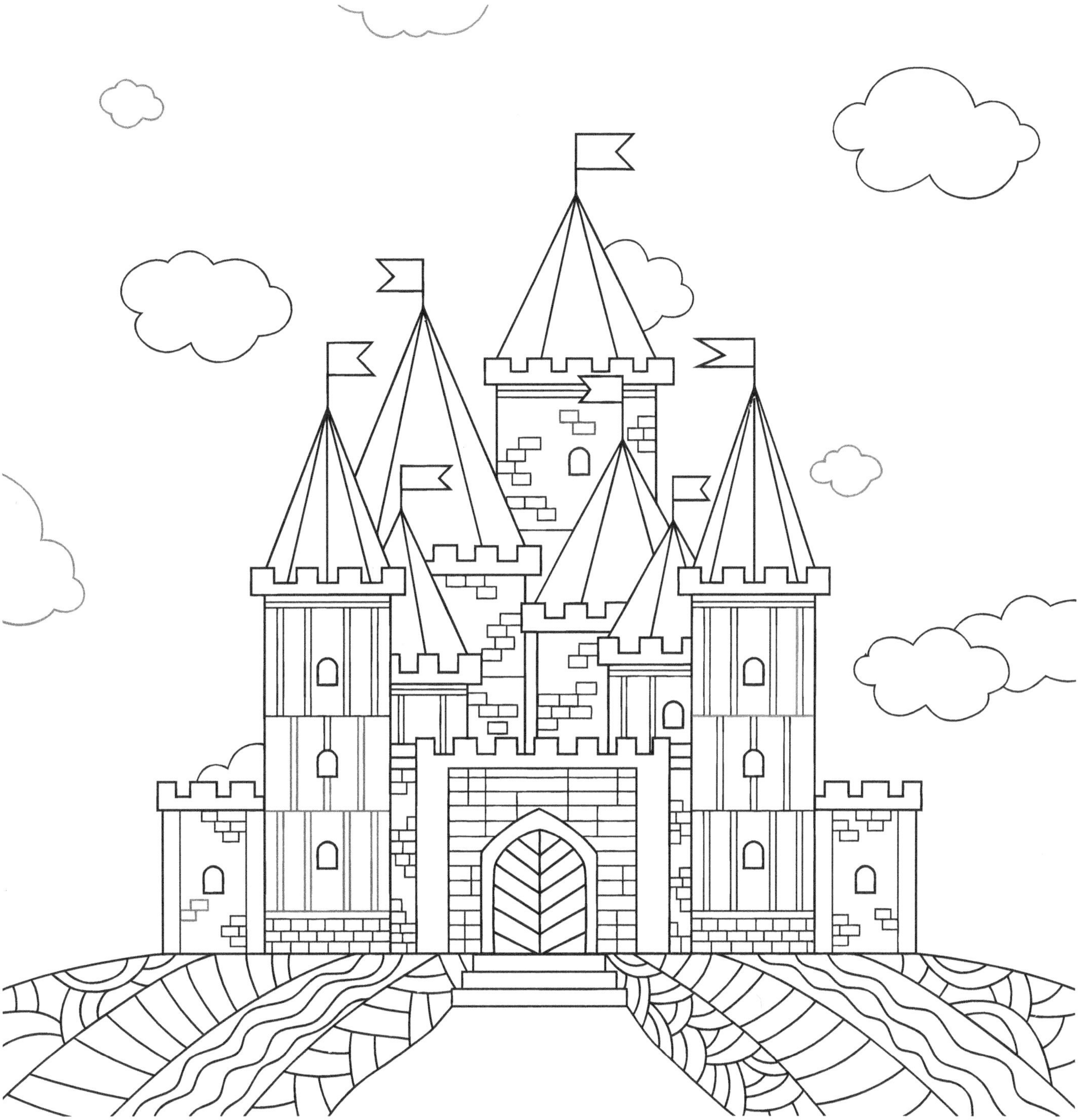

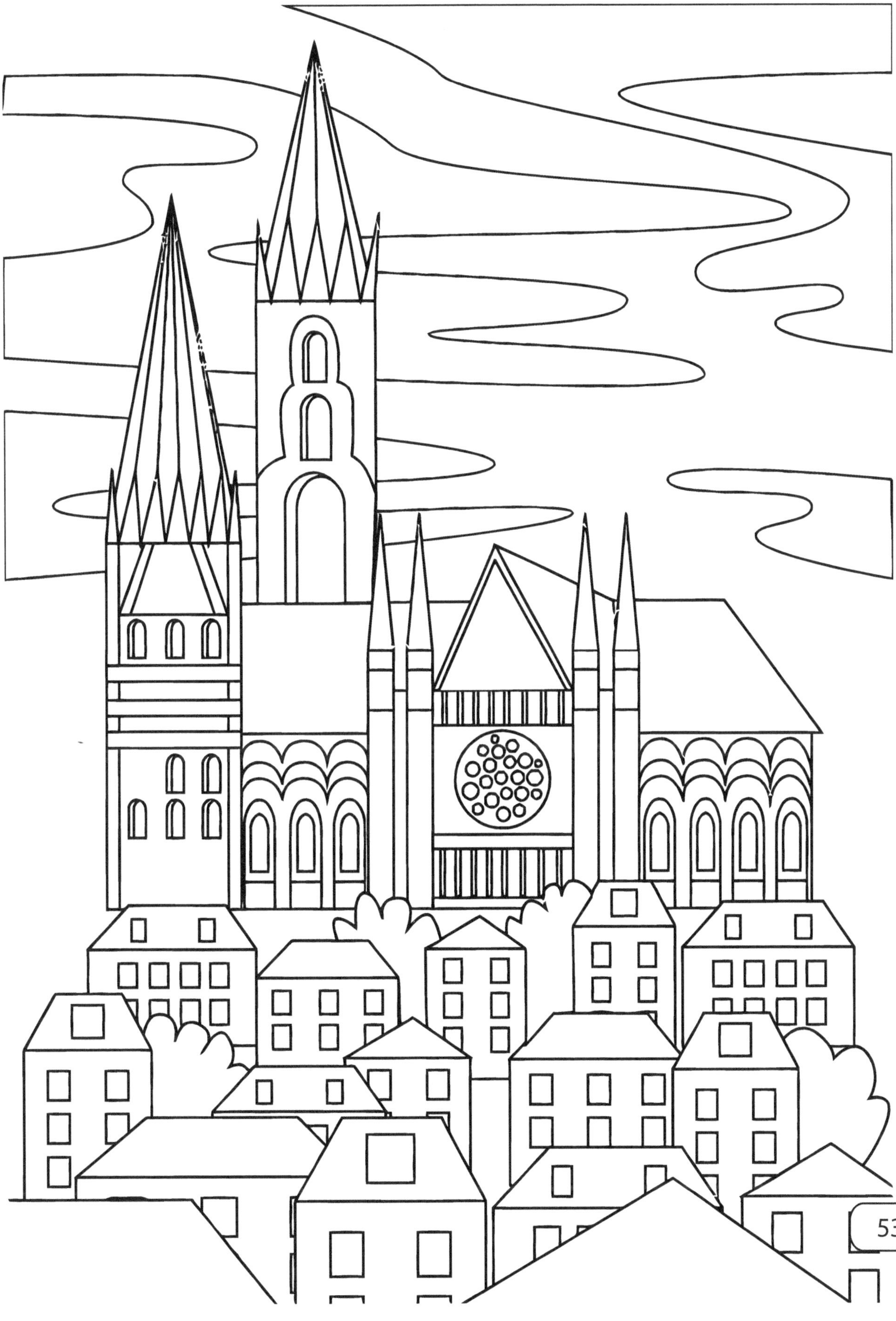

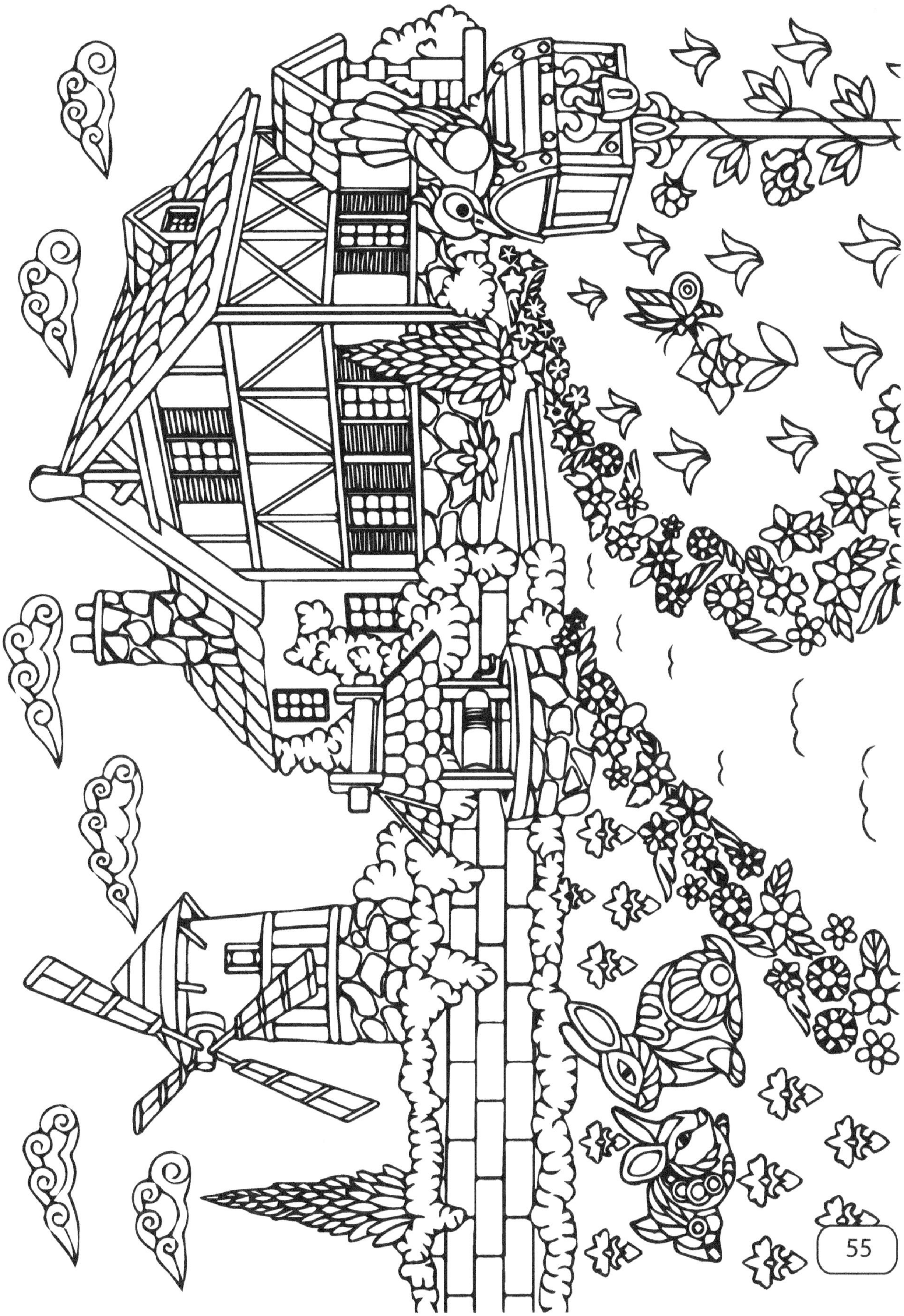

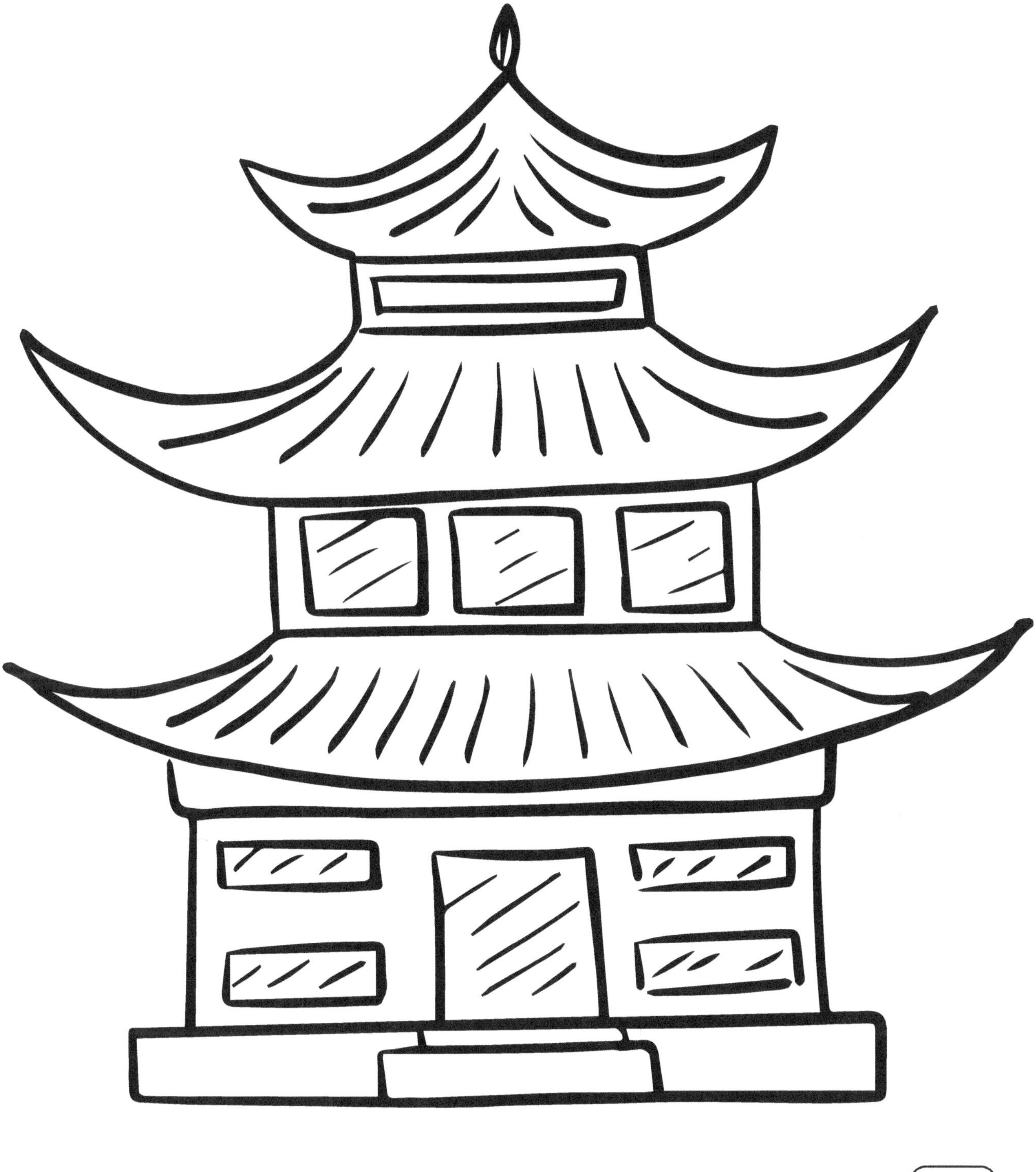

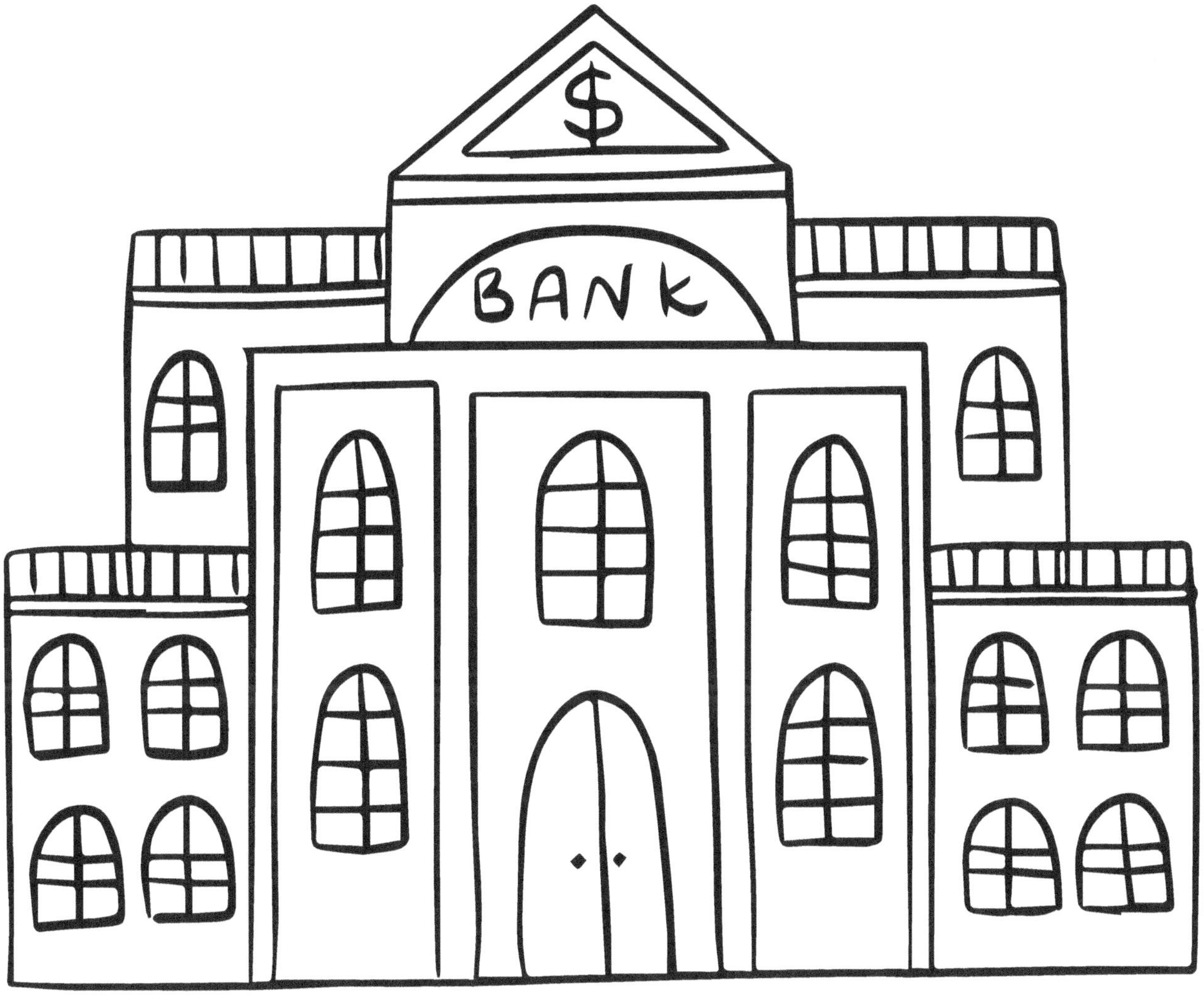
$
BANK

www.ingramcontent.com/pod-product-compliance
Lightning Source LLC
Chambersburg PA
CBHW080951220526
45465CB00008BA/3245